# Construction Defects 101

# The Definitive Guide to Understanding Construction Defects in California

By Scott Levine, Esq.

SCOTT LEVINE

*Copyright ©2016 Scott Levine*

ISBN – 10:098626511x
ISBN – 13-978-0-9862651-1-2

## Table of Contents

# Chapter 1

# Introduction

What is a Construction Defect?  How can I get help with construction defects?  Who can help me?  What is it going to cost?  How do I pay for help?  Why am I stuck in this situation in the first place?

These are all good questions and common questions that are asked by homeowners and the members of boards of directors. Often times construction defects are discovered because of a leak after it rains or because something seems to need a lot of repairs and it still is not working right.  Other times you become aware of construction defects because your property manager tells you that you need to do an investigation.  Sometimes you find out from your neighbors or from an attorney who was contacted by your neighbors.

**What is a Construction Defect?**

If your home was built before 2003, a construction defect was defined by the common law.  That meant that you would need to satisfy the elements of a strict liability or a negligence cause of action.  In general, a defect had to cause damage to something else.  Thus, if a window leaked but only damaged the window itself, there was no cause of action.  Since this did not make sense, legislation followed to cure this problem.

In 2002, the California Legislature passed what is known as SB800. SB stands for Senate Bill and 800 is the bill number.  In short, SB800 created a statute that homeowners and homeowner associations can use to define and bring construction defect claims.

In general, the statute has 2 parts.  One part covers the pre-litigation procedures that must be followed.  The other part covers "standards" or the definition of what is a construction defect.

With these definitions or "standards" it is easier to determine if a problem fits the definition of a construction defect.  If the problem is not listed in the standards but it does cause damage (as under the common law), it may still be considered a construction defect.  Following the listed standards, there is a catchall section for defects that cause damage.

**How can I get help with construction defects?**

The statute provides that a pre-litigation claim under the statute must be identified as a claim pursuant to Civil Code §910.  If you simply call customer service, the timelines set forth in the statute do not come into play.  The statute is set up to allow you to make your own claim.  That said, most homeowners and homeowner associations hire a lawyer who concentrates their practice handling construction defect claims.

There is no recognized specialty by the State Bar of California but construction defect litigation is an area that requires some specialized knowledge.  If you are going to get help, you should hire a lawyer or a law firm that handles these types of cases, rather than a general practitioner.

**Who can help me?**

Scott Levine was one of the principle drafters and negotiators of SB800.  He spent numerous days in Sacramento during the summer of 2002 working with the California Building Industry Association and the Building Industry Association lawyers and lobbyists developing the statute.  The law was for the most part written by the people in the day to day negotiations.  The Legislature provided several members of the Assembly and

Senate to assist in the negotiations. Once a point was agreed upon, drafts were created and exchanged. Follow-up meetings were held and ultimately, SB800 was passed on the floors of both the Assembly and Senate in late August 2002.

Scott Levine was chosen to be one of the two attorney leaders involved in the day to day negotiations because he has been a construction defect litigator for over 20 years. This experience has given him the ability to see firsthand the problems that the common law posed. It also afforded him the ability to understand the purpose of the "right to repair" and the ways that builders would, if they could, abuse it to delay the process.

**What is it going to cost? How do I pay for help?**

Construction Defect cases can be handled by a lawyer on an a hourly; contingency fee; or a split or blended hourly/contingency fee basis.

**Hourly Fees**
When a lawyer handles a case on an hourly basis, you will be charged for each hour that the lawyer and/or its staff works on the case. Generally, you will receive a bill each month. The bill will also include investigation expenses, which will be due and payable when you receive the bill.

**Contingency Fees**
When a lawyer handles a case on a contingency fee basis, you will not be billed for the time that they spend during the case. Instead, you will pay the lawyer, from a settlement or other recovery. The recovery can be in the form of cash from the developer and/or from the value of repairs that are made by the developer/builder during the pre-litigation process.

In addition to the fees charged, you will also be charged for the investigation expenses. These charges can be deducted either before or after the attorney fees are deducted. Whether a lawyer will handle a case on a net or gross contingency fee depends on the case and other factors.

**Split Contingency Fee**
This is a fee that often entails ½ hourly and ½ contingency. You can slide the percentages to fit whatever you and your lawyer agree upon before the engagement begins.

Regardless of how a lawyer is paid, you should require that experts provide budgets before they get started. When experts don't provide budgets, the costs of the investigation are generally higher. Regardless of the way they are deducted from the recovery, it is still money that the homeowner or the association pays. Thus it is important that you be aware of the costs as they are incurred so that you are not surprised at the end of the case.

**Why am I stuck in this situation in the first place?**

This is a good question and you should not feel bad. You have construction defects because most construction in California has them. It is not something that you, your realtor or even the home inspector you hired could have found. Most of the problems occur after rain or a series of rains. Some problems develop as products used by builders don't work as intended.

While most builders don't want to build projects with defects, the problems arise because of the subcontractors that are hired as well as the lack of supervision and/or coordination of the trades.

The whole project is generally built with time as the main factor. Builders want to finish projects as quickly as they can so that they can sell them before the market turns downward. Subcontractors bid their work by the job, not the hour. Thus, subcontractors want to get the work done quicker.

This all leads to a recipe of construction defects. Some builders are better with post-construction problems than others.

However, most builders use customer service representatives to coordinate repairs that often are simply a cover-up of the real problem. It is not that they are bad people, rather they don't have the time or ability to investigate the problems and offer a proper solution.

Because of these factors, most homes, condominiums and townhomes will be the subject of construction defects. If you are in a rare project that is approaching 10 years without apparent problems, you should not wait for the 10-year mark to pass before at least inquiring of a construction defect attorney. Another mistake is to hire a general contractor to do a review of the project. While a general contractor that works with construction defect attorneys may be qualified to do this investigation, you are still better off working with a lawyer that handles these types of cases. In most situations, we will perform this initial investigation and meeting with homeowners and/or board members free of charge and without obligation.

If your home and/or association is approaching the 10-year mark call us. If your home and/or association is having recurring problems or you think you may have construction defects, call us. We will be happy to talk to you and come out to your home or association to see what you are seeing. From that point, we can discuss your options and advise you going forward.

SCOTT LEVINE

# Chapter 2

# The History of Construction Defects in California

California is a consumer friendly state. Since the 1960s, the California Supreme Court has handed down decisions that explain how and why consumers should be able to pursue manufacturers and those in the chain of distribution for injuries.

In 1969, the California Supreme Court handed down its first decision that extended consumer products liability law to homes. The case was entitled *Kriegler v. Eichler Homes (1969) 269 Cal. App. 2d 224*. The Court reasoned that homes in California, much like other products made on an assembly line, are similar. Homes in California are built on an assembly line of sorts. Several "models" are designed and then from those "models" numerous homes are built to replicate the "model" home shown to the prospective purchaser.

Later that same year, the Court of Appeal handed down its decision in *Avner v. Longridge Estates (1969) 272 Cal. App. 2d 607.* In that decision, the Court held that the developer of mass produced lots too was strictly liable. The Court reasoned that a developer did not necessarily have to build the house but if it mass produced lots it too would be held strictly liable for defects in the lot(s).

From 1969 until 2000, much of the focus of construction defect litigation centered upon how a builder could or could not pass its liability on to its subcontractors. Often these were contract cases but they also involved indemnity – the passing of liability from one party to a more culpable or responsible party for the loss.

Some exceptions are found in the following cases:

### Stearman v. Centex Homes (2000) 78 Cal. App. 4th 611

In this case, the Court held that homeowners and/or Associations are entitled to recover their investigation costs from defendants in construction defect actions. The Court reasoned that investigation costs are an element of damages suffered by a homeowner and/or an Association. This element of damage was later codified in Civil Code §944.

### Casey v. Overhead Door Corporation (1999) 74 Cal. App. 4th 112

In this case, the owners of mass produced homes sought to hold the subcontractor who supplied and installed defective garage doors strictly liable. The trial court denied this claim and the Court of Appeal agreed.

This decision was effectively reversed by the California Supreme Court's decision 3 years later in **Jiminez v. Superior Court (2002) 29 Cal. 4th 473**. In *Jiminez*, the California Supreme Court reasoned that a manufacturer of windows is similar to the manufacturer of other products and thus subject to strict liability. This decision was pending while SB800 was being negotiated. A provision in Civil Code §936 makes reference to the fact that if a party is subject to strict liability under the common law, it is subject to the no fault standard that applies to a builder.

### Windham At Carmel Mountain Ranch Assn. v. Superior Court (2003) 109 Cal. App. 4th 1162.

This case held that an Association is entitled to recover under the theory of Implied Warranty. This is an important decision even today as the statutory cause of action carves out an exception for warranty claims. Thus, many courts have held (since the inception of SB800) that Associations may properly maintain a cause of action for Breach of Implied Warranty.

### Raven's Cove Townhomes, Inc. v. Knuppe Development Co. (1981) 114 Cal. App. 3d 783.

In this case, the Court held a builder liable for failure to properly fund the Association's reserve account. In development there is an inherent conflict between the builder and the setting of a proper assessment. The higher the assessment, the lower the selling price. Thus, builders often set assessments low. Years later, the Association realizes that its reserves are insufficient and that for many years it was underfunding its reserves. This case can be used to hold a builder liable for this failure and the resulting shortfall in the reserves.

In 2000, the California Supreme Court handed down its decision *Aas v. Superior Court (2000) 24 Cal. 4th 627*. This decision effectively ended the ability of homeowners and Associations from being able to recover for defective conditions that had not yet caused damage. Thus, if a roof was installed wrong and would leak and/or be damaged in the future, if it did not get damaged before the statute of limitations expired, the homeowner would be stuck with the defect and its resulting damage. The Court argued that the common law which evolved from strict products liability had long ago held that pure economic loss (damage to the product itself) was not recoverable. Thus, because strict liability for homes evolved from the same line of cases, the Court was powerless to extend the doctrine. It called for the legislature to pass legislation if it was so inclined to change the state of the law.

In 2002 builders and representatives from the Consumer Attorneys of California met from May to the end of August and worked out a new law. The bill that was being negotiated was very complicated and involved members of the California Building Industry Association, the Building Industry Association, and the Insurance Federation on one side with the Consumer Attorneys of California on the other side.

The issues were complex but in the end there were two goals that the parties wanted to achieve. Builders wanted a right to repair. Homeowners wanted the ability to sue for violations of standards before they caused damage.

This backdrop lead us to SB800 in the end of the legislative session of 2002.

In addition, the following cases concern construction defects today, along with the statute.

***Seahuas La Jolla Owners Assn v. Superior Court (2014) 224 Cal. App. 4th 754.*** In this case, the attorney-client privilege was challenged by the builder. The attorney who represented the Association provided periodic updates to the membership. The builder argued that the updates were not privileged because the members were not the client of the attorney. The Court disagreed and found that attorney updates to the members of the Association it represents are in fact protected by the Attorney-Client privilege.

***Beacon Residential Community Association v. Skidmore, Owings & Merrill LLP (2014) 59 Cal. 4th 568.*** Before this case was handed down by the California Supreme Court, homeowners and Associations were not able to sue architects directly for their failure to properly design their homes/buildings. Cases held before Beacon that an architect owed a duty to its customer – the developer – not the ultimate homeowner. This case changed that and homeowners and Associations are able to sue architects for beach of their duty of care to the ultimate owner or occupant of the home.

***Market Lofts Community Association v. 9th Street Market Lofts, LLC (2014) 222 Cal. App. 4th 924.*** This case provides that an Association can sue on its behalf as well as on behalf of its members in a "representative" action. This is similar to a "class action" but is authorized by statute – See Civil Code §5980. Sometimes builders cause damage to the rights of homeowners that are impossible to bring as lawsuits on an individualized basis. This case allows for bringing these cases on a "representative" basis. It is also likely that an Association could act as the Class Representative in a Class Action on behalf of its members.

***Pinnacle Museum Tower Association v. Pinnacle Market Development (US), LLC (2012) 55 Cal. 4th 223***. This case was a lawsuit that was filed in San Diego Superior Court. The builder moved to compel or force the Association into arbitration. The Superior Court denied the request and the builder took the issue up on appeal. The Court of Appeal agreed with the Trial Court. The builder appealed to the California Supreme Court which reversed both the Court of Appeal and the Trial Court. The Supreme Court held that an arbitration clause included in a development's CC&Rs is enforceable under certain circumstances. In this case, it concerned a Federal Arbitration Act clause. The Court held that this particular clause was enforceable in a later construction defect claim.

Prior to the Pinnacle decision, another decision wound its way through the Courts. ***Treo @ Kettner Homeowners Association v. Superior Court (2008) 166 Cal. App. 4th 1055***. This decision declined to allow a builder to enforce a Judicial Reference clause in its CC&Rs. Of interest is that the Pinnacle Court failed to extend its decision to Judicial References. Thus, it is arguable that the only type of arbitration clause that is enforceable in a set of CC&Rs is a Federal Arbitration Act Arbitration Clause.

SCOTT LEVINE

# Chapter 3

# SB800 – Standards for Construction and Claims Procedures.

SB800 is divided into 5 chapters. These Chapters work in conjunction with the other chapters. In general, the chapters are as follows:

### Chapter 1 – Definitions

In this Chapter, you will find what words used in the statute mean. It is important that you use these definitions as they are used in the statute because they are not what they may mean in other common uses or language. For example, close of escrow seems like a simple term. However, if you read the definition, it is defined to occur at a certain date or when certain events happen if you are a homeowner association.

### Chapter 2 – Actionable Defects

In this Chapter, you will find the standards for construction. Using the definitions, you will learn what roofs, windows, doors and other parts of your home and/or common area are to be built to withstand. The standards vary depending upon the component. Some items, like plumbing, have multiple types of standards.

In addition, you will see that the standards have in general a 10-year statute of limitations. Some standards though have shorter timelines. Some as little as 1 year and others with other limits between 3 and 5 years.

### Chapter 3 – Obligations

The statute provides that a builder can offer a pre-litigation procedure that is different than what is set forth in Chapter 4. In addition, the statute provides certain minimum standards and timelines for those standards. If the pre-litigation procedure is more onerous on the homeowner or association than what is offered in Chapter 4, it may not be enforceable. In order to understand whether or not the alternative pre-litigation procedure is or is not enforceable, you should consult with a construction defect attorney.

## Chapter 4 – Pre-Litigation Procedures

This Chapter sets forth the timelines and procedures for homeowners, associations and builders. If a builder wants to make repairs, there are strict timelines. If a homeowner or an association wants to stay within the strict timelines there are items and events that it must allow the builder to follow/attend. If a homeowner or an association fails to allow a builder the opportunity to make repairs within this Chapter, a homeowner and/or an association can lose its right to recover for the defect altogether.

## Chapter 5 – Procedure

This Chapter defines the damages that a homeowner and/or an association can recover. It also lists the affirmative defenses available to a builder and/or its subcontractors.

Together, these Chapters set forth the pre-litigation and litigation procedures and standards for construction defects in California. If you are a Homeowners Association, there are often additional requirements that you must follow. These requirements can be found in your governing documents (CC&Rs and Bylaws) as well as within the Davis-Sterling Act (§§6000 and 6100).

# Chapter 4

# SB800 – The Statute

## Table of Contents – SB800

## Chapter 1 - Definitions

### § 895. Definitions

(a) "Structure" means any residential dwelling, other building, or improvement located upon a lot or within a common area.

(b) "Designed moisture barrier" means an installed moisture barrier specified in the plans and specifications, contract documents, or manufacturer's recommendations.

(c) "Actual moisture barrier" means any component or material, actually installed, that serves to any degree as a barrier against moisture, whether or not intended as a barrier against moisture.

(d) "Unintended water" means water that passes beyond, around, or through a component or the material that is designed to prevent that passage.

(e) "Close of escrow" means the date of the close of escrow between the builder and the original homeowner. With respect to claims by an association, as defined in Section 4080, "close of escrow" means the date of substantial completion, as defined in Section 337.15 of the Code of Civil Procedure, or the date the builder relinquishes control over the association's ability to decide whether to initiate a claim under this title, whichever is later.

(f) "Claimant" or "homeowner" includes the individual owners of single-family homes, individual unit owners of attached dwellings and, in the case of a common interest development, any association as defined in Section 4080.

## Chapter 2 – Actionable Defects

### § 896. Building standards for original construction intended to be sold as an individual dwelling unit

In any action seeking recovery of damages arising out of, or related to deficiencies in, the residential construction, design, specifications, surveying, planning, supervision, testing, or observation of construction, a builder, and to the extent set forth in Chapter 4 (commencing with Section 910), a general contractor, subcontractor, material supplier, individual product manufacturer, or design professional, shall, except as specifically set forth in this title, be liable for, and the claimant's claims or causes of action shall be limited to violation of, the following standards, except as specifically set forth in this title. This title applies to original construction intended to be sold as an individual dwelling unit. As to condominium conversions, this title does not apply to or does not supersede any other statutory or common law.

(a) With respect to water issues:

(1) A door shall not allow unintended water to pass beyond, around, or through the door or its designed or actual moisture barriers, if any.

(2) Windows, patio doors, deck doors, and their systems shall not allow water to pass beyond, around, or through the window, patio door, or deck door or its designed or actual moisture barriers, including, without limitation, internal barriers within the systems themselves. For purposes of this paragraph, "systems" include, without limitation, windows, window assemblies, framing, substrate, flashings, and trim, if any.

(3) Windows, patio doors, deck doors, and their systems shall not allow excessive condensation to enter the structure and cause damage to another component. For purposes of this paragraph, "systems" include, without limitation, windows, window assemblies, framing, substrate, flashings, and trim, if any.

(4) Roofs, roofing systems, chimney caps, and ventilation components shall not allow water to enter the structure or to pass beyond, around, or through the designed or actual moisture barriers, including, without limitation, internal barriers located within the systems themselves. For purposes of this paragraph, "systems" include, without limitation, framing, substrate, and sheathing, if any.

(5) Decks, deck systems, balconies, balcony systems, exterior stairs, and stair systems shall not allow water to pass into the adjacent structure. For purposes of this paragraph, "systems" include, without limitation, framing, substrate, flashing, and sheathing, if any.

(6) Decks, deck systems, balconies, balcony systems, exterior stairs, and stair systems shall not allow unintended water to pass within the systems themselves and cause damage to the systems. For purposes of this paragraph, "systems" include, without limitation, framing, substrate, flashing, and sheathing, if any.

(7) Foundation systems and slabs shall not allow water or vapor to enter into the structure so as to cause damage to another building component.

(8) Foundation systems and slabs shall not allow water or vapor to enter into the structure so as to limit the installation of the type of flooring materials typically used for the particular application.

(9) Hardscape, including paths and patios, irrigation systems, landscaping

systems, and drainage systems, that are installed as part of the original construction, shall not be installed in such a way as to cause water or soil erosion to enter into or come in contact with the structure so as to cause damage to another building component.

(10) Stucco, exterior siding, exterior walls, including, without limitation, exterior framing, and other exterior wall finishes and fixtures and the systems of those components and fixtures, including, but not limited to, pot shelves, horizontal surfaces, columns, and plant-ons, shall be installed in such a way so as not to allow unintended water to pass into the structure or to pass beyond, around, or through the designed or actual moisture barriers of the system, including any internal barriers located within the system itself. For purposes of this paragraph, "systems" include, without limitation, framing, substrate, flashings, trim, wall assemblies, and internal wall cavities, if any.

(11) Stucco, exterior siding, and exterior walls shall not allow excessive condensation to enter the structure and cause damage to another component. For purposes of this paragraph, "systems" include, without limitation, framing, substrate, flashings, trim, wall assemblies, and internal wall cavities, if any.

(12) Retaining and site walls and their associated drainage systems shall not allow unintended water to pass beyond, around, or through its designed or actual moisture barriers including, without limitation, any internal barriers, so as to cause damage. This standard does not apply to those portions of any wall or drainage system that are designed to have water flow beyond, around, or through them.

(13) Retaining walls and site walls, and their associated drainage systems, shall only allow water to flow beyond, around, or through the areas designated by design.

(14) The lines and components of the plumbing system, sewer system, and utility systems shall not leak.

(15) Plumbing lines, sewer lines, and utility lines shall not corrode so as to impede the useful life of the systems.

(16) Sewer systems shall be installed in such a way as to allow the designated amount of sewage to flow through the system.

(17) Showers, baths, and related waterproofing systems shall not leak water into the interior of walls, flooring systems, or the interior of other components.

(18) The waterproofing system behind or under ceramic tile and tile countertops shall not allow water into the interior of walls, flooring systems, or other components so as to cause damage. Ceramic tile systems shall be designed and installed so as to deflect intended water to the waterproofing system.

(b) With respect to structural issues:

(1) Foundations, load bearing components, and slabs, shall not contain significant cracks or significant vertical displacement.

(2) Foundations, load bearing components, and slabs shall not cause the structure, in whole or in part, to be structurally unsafe.

(3) Foundations, load bearing components, and slabs, and underlying soils shall be constructed so as to materially comply with the design criteria set by applicable government building codes, regulations, and ordinances for chemical deterioration or corrosion resistance in effect at the time of original construction.

(4) A structure shall be constructed so as to materially comply with the design criteria for earthquake and wind load resistance, as set forth in the applicable government building codes, regulations, and ordinances in effect at the time of original construction.

(c) With respect to soil issues:

(1) Soils and engineered retaining walls shall not cause, in whole or in part, damage to the structure built upon the soil or engineered retaining wall.

(2) Soils and engineered retaining walls shall not cause, in whole or in part, the structure to be structurally unsafe.

(3) Soils shall not cause, in whole or in part, the land upon which no structure is built to become unusable for the purpose represented at the time of original sale by the builder or for the purpose for which that land is commonly used.

(d) With respect to fire protection issues:

(1) A structure shall be constructed so as to materially comply with the design criteria of the applicable government building codes, regulations, and ordinances for fire protection of the occupants in effect at the time of the original construction.

(2) Fireplaces, chimneys, chimney structures, and chimney termination caps shall be constructed and installed in such a way so as not to cause an unreasonable risk of fire outside the fireplace enclosure or chimney.

(3) Electrical and mechanical systems shall be constructed and installed in such a way so as not to cause an unreasonable risk of fire.

(e) With respect to plumbing and sewer issues:

Plumbing and sewer systems shall be installed to operate properly and shall not materially impair the use of the structure by its inhabitants. However, no action may be brought for a violation of this subdivision more than four years after close of escrow.

(f) With respect to electrical system issues:

Electrical systems shall operate properly and shall not materially impair the use of the structure by its inhabitants. However, no action shall be brought pursuant to this subdivision more than four years from close of escrow.

(g) With respect to issues regarding other areas of construction:

(1) Exterior pathways, driveways, hardscape, sidewalls, sidewalks, and patios installed by the original builder shall not contain cracks that display significant vertical displacement or that are excessive. However, no action shall be brought upon a violation of this paragraph more than four years from close of escrow.

(2) Stucco, exterior siding, and other exterior wall finishes and fixtures, including, but not limited to, pot shelves, horizontal surfaces, columns, and plant-ons, shall not contain significant cracks or separations.

(3)(A) To the extent not otherwise covered by these standards, manufactured products, including, but not limited to, windows, doors, roofs, plumbing products and fixtures, fireplaces, electrical fixtures, HVAC units, countertops, cabinets, paint, and appliances shall be installed so as not to interfere with the products' useful life, if any.

(B) For purposes of this paragraph, "useful life" means a representation of how long a product is warranted or represented, through its limited warranty or any written representations, to last by its manufacturer, including recommended or required maintenance. If there is no representation by a manufacturer, a builder shall install manufactured products so as not to interfere with the product's utility.

(C) For purposes of this paragraph, "manufactured product" means a product that is completely manufactured offsite.

(D) If no useful life representation is made, or if the representation is less than one year, the period shall be no less than one year. If a manufactured product is damaged as a result of a violation of these standards, damage to the product is a recoverable element of damages. This subparagraph does not limit recovery if there has been damage to another building component caused by a manufactured product during the manufactured product's useful life.

(E) This title does not apply in any action seeking recovery solely for a defect in a manufactured product located within or adjacent to a structure.

(4) Heating shall be installed so as to be capable of maintaining a room temperature of 70 degrees Fahrenheit at a point three feet above the floor in any living space if the heating was installed pursuant to a building permit application submitted prior to January 1, 2008, or capable of maintaining a room temperature of 68 degrees Fahrenheit at a point three feet above the floor and two feet from exterior walls in all habitable rooms at the design temperature if the heating was installed pursuant to a building permit application submitted on or before January 1, 2008.

(5) Living space air-conditioning, if any, shall be provided in a manner consistent with the size and efficiency design criteria specified in Title 24 of the California Code of Regulations or its successor.

(6) Attached structures shall be constructed to comply with interunit noise transmission standards set by the applicable government building codes, ordinances, or regulations in effect at the time of the original construction. If there is no applicable code, ordinance, or regulation, this paragraph does not apply. However, no action shall be brought pursuant to this paragraph more than one year from the original occupancy of the adjacent unit.

(7) Irrigation systems and drainage shall operate properly so as not to damage landscaping or other external improvements. However, no action shall be brought pursuant to this paragraph more than one year from close of escrow.

(8) Untreated wood posts shall not be installed in contact with soil so as to cause unreasonable decay to the wood based upon the finish grade at the time of original construction. However, no action shall be brought pursuant to this paragraph more than two years from close of escrow.

(9) Untreated steel fences and adjacent components shall be installed so as to prevent unreasonable corrosion. However, no action shall be brought pursuant to this paragraph more than four years from close of escrow.

(10) Paint and stains shall be applied in such a manner so as not to cause deterioration of the building surfaces for the length of time specified by the paint or stain manufacturers' representations, if any. However, no action shall be brought pursuant to this paragraph more than five years from close of escrow.

(11) Roofing materials shall be installed so as to avoid materials falling from the roof.

(12) The landscaping systems shall be installed in such a manner so as to survive for not less than one year. However, no action shall be brought pursuant to this paragraph more than two years from close of escrow.

(13) Ceramic tile and tile backing shall be installed in such a manner that the

tile does not detach.

(14) Dryer ducts shall be installed and terminated pursuant to manufacturer installation requirements. However, no action shall be brought pursuant to this paragraph more than two years from close of escrow.

(15) Structures shall be constructed in such a manner so as not to impair the occupants' safety because they contain public health hazards as determined by a duly authorized public health official, health agency, or governmental entity having jurisdiction. This paragraph does not limit recovery for any damages caused by a violation of any other paragraph of this section on the grounds that the damages do not constitute a health hazard.

## § 897. Function or component of a structure; scope of standards within chapter

The standards set forth in this chapter are intended to address every function or component of a structure. To the extent that a function or component of a structure is not addressed by these standards, it shall be actionable if it causes damage.

## Chapter 3 - Obligations

## § 900. Fit and finish; limited warranty; scope

As to fit and finish items, a builder shall provide a homebuyer with a minimum one-year express written limited warranty covering the fit and finish of the following building components. Except as otherwise provided by the standards specified in Chapter 2 (commencing with Section 896), this warranty shall cover the fit and finish of cabinets, mirrors, flooring, interior and exterior walls, countertops, paint finishes, and trim, but shall not apply to damage to those components caused by defects in other components governed by the other provisions of this title. Any fit and finish matters covered by this warranty are not subject to the provisions of this title. If a builder fails to provide the express warranty required by this section, the warranty for these items shall be for a period of one year.

## § 901. Enhanced protection agreement; length of time; minimum standards

A builder may, but is not required to, offer greater protection or protection for longer time periods in its express contract with the homeowner than that set forth in Chapter 2 (commencing with Section 896). A builder may not limit the application of Chapter 2 (commencing with Section 896) or lower its protection through the express contract with the homeowner. This type of express contract constitutes an "enhanced protection agreement."

## § 902. Enhanced protection agreement; determination of enforceability

If a builder offers an enhanced protection agreement, the builder may choose to be subject to its own express contractual provisions in place of the provisions set forth in Chapter 2 (commencing with Section 896). If an enhanced protection agreement is in place, Chapter 2 (commencing with Section 896) no longer applies other than to set forth minimum provisions by which to judge the enforceability of the particular provisions of the enhanced protection agreement.

## § 903. Enhanced protection agreement; time to elect agreement; standards where provisions are unenforceable

If a builder offers an enhanced protection agreement in place of the provisions set forth in Chapter 2 (commencing with Section 896), the election to do so shall be made in writing with the homeowner no later than the close of escrow. The builder shall provide the homeowner with a complete copy of Chapter 2 (commencing with Section 896) and advise the homeowner that the builder has elected not to be subject to its provisions. If any provision of an enhanced protection agreement is later found to be unenforceable as not meeting the minimum standards of Chapter 2 (commencing with Section 896), a builder may use this chapter in lieu of those provisions found to be unenforceable.

## § 904. Enhanced protection agreement; disputed terms; notice of claim against builder

If a builder has elected to use an enhanced protection agreement, and a homeowner disputes that the particular provision or time periods of the enhanced protection agreement are not greater than, or equal to, the provisions of Chapter 2 (commencing with Section 896) as they apply to the particular deficiency alleged by the homeowner, the homeowner may seek to enforce the application of the standards set forth in this chapter as to those claimed deficiencies. If a homeowner seeks to enforce a particular standard in lieu of a provision of the enhanced protection agreement, the homeowner shall give the builder written notice of that intent at the time the homeowner files a notice of claim pursuant to Chapter 4 (commencing with Section 910).

## § 905. Enhanced protection agreement; binding determination of applicable building standards; waiver; privity with nonoriginal homeowners

If a homeowner seeks to enforce Chapter 2 (commencing with Section 896), in lieu of the enhanced protection agreement in a subsequent litigation or other legal action, the builder shall have the right to have the matter bifurcated, and to have an immediately binding determination of his or her responsive pleading within 60 days after the filing of that pleading, but in no event after the commencement of discovery, as to the application of either Chapter 2 (commencing with Section 896) or the enhanced protection agreement as to the deficiencies claimed by the homeowner. If the builder fails to seek that determination in the timeframe specified, the builder waives the right to do so and the standards set forth in this title shall apply. As to any nonoriginal homeowner, that homeowner shall be deemed in privity for purposes of an enhanced protection agreement only to the extent that the builder has recorded the enhanced protection agreement on title or provided actual notice to the nonoriginal homeowner of the enhanced protection agreement. If the enhanced protection agreement is not recorded on title or no actual notice has been provided, the standards set forth in this title apply to any nonoriginal homeowners' claims.

## § 906. Prelitigation procedures; governing law

A builder's election to use an enhanced protection agreement addresses only the issues set forth in Chapter 2 (commencing with Section 896) and does not constitute an election to use or not use the provisions of Chapter 4 (commencing with Section 910). The decision to use or not use Chapter 4 (commencing with Section 910) is governed by the provisions of that chapter.

## § 907. Homeowner maintenance obligations, schedules and practices

A homeowner is obligated to follow all reasonable maintenance obligations and schedules communicated in writing to the homeowner by the builder and product manufacturers, as well as commonly accepted maintenance practices. A failure by a homeowner to follow these obligations, schedules, and practices may subject the homeowner to the affirmative defenses contained in Section 944.

## Chapter 4 – Prelitigation Procedure

## § 910. Written notice of claim

Prior to filing an action against any party alleged to have contributed to a violation of the standards set forth in Chapter 2 (commencing with Section 896), the claimant shall initiate the following prelitigation procedures:

(a) The claimant or his or her legal representative shall provide written notice via certified mail, overnight mail, or personal delivery to the builder, in the manner prescribed in this section, of the claimant's claim that the construction of his or her residence violates any of the standards set forth in Chapter 2 (commencing with Section 896). That notice shall provide the claimant's name, address, and preferred method of contact, and shall state that the claimant alleges a violation pursuant to this part against the builder, and shall describe the claim in reasonable detail sufficient to determine the nature and location, to the extent known, of the claimed violation. In the case of a group of homeowners or an association, the notice may identify the claimants solely by address or other description sufficient to apprise the builder of the locations of the subject residences. That document shall have the same force and effect as a notice of commencement of a legal proceeding.

(b) The notice requirements of this section do not preclude a homeowner from seeking redress through any applicable normal customer service procedure as set forth in any contractual, warranty, or other builder-generated document; and, if a homeowner seeks to do so, that request shall not satisfy the notice requirements of this section.

## § 911. "Builder" defined

(a) For purposes of this title, except as provided in subdivision (b), "builder" means any entity or individual, including, but not limited to a builder, developer, general contractor, contractor, or original seller, who, at the time of sale, was also in the business of selling residential units to the public for the property that is the subject of the homeowner's claim or was in the business of building, developing, or constructing residential units for public purchase for the property that is the subject of the homeowner's claim.

(b) For the purposes of this title, "builder" does not include any entity or individual whose involvement with a residential unit that is the subject of the homeowner's claim is limited to his or her capacity as general contractor or contractor and who is not a partner, member of, subsidiary of, or otherwise similarly affiliated with the builder. For purposes of this title, these nonaffiliated general contractors and nonaffiliated contractors shall be treated the same as subcontractors, material suppliers, individual product manufacturers, and design professionals.

## § 912. Document disclosure by builder; designated agent to accept claims and act on builder's behalf; notice to homeowners and purchasers

A builder shall do all of the following:

(a) Within 30 days of a written request by a homeowner or his or her legal representative, the builder shall provide copies of all relevant plans, specifications, mass or rough grading plans, final soils reports, Bureau of Real Estate public reports, and available engineering calculations, that pertain to a homeowner's residence specifically or as part of a larger development tract. The request shall be honored if it states that it is made relative to structural, fire safety, or soils provisions of this title. However, a builder is not obligated to provide a copying service, and reasonable copying costs shall be borne by the requesting party. A builder may require that the documents be copied onsite by the requesting party, except that the homeowner may, at his or her option, use his or her own copying service, which may include an offsite copy facility that is bonded and insured. If a builder can show that the builder maintained the documents, but that they later became unavailable due to loss or destruction that was not the fault of the builder, the builder may be excused from the requirements of this subdivision, in which case the builder shall act with reasonable diligence to assist the homeowner in obtaining those documents from any applicable government authority or from the source that generated the document. However, in that case, the time limits specified by this section do not apply.

(b) At the expense of the homeowner, who may opt to use an offsite copy facility that is bonded and insured, the builder shall provide to the homeowner or his or her legal representative copies of all maintenance and preventative maintenance recommendations that pertain to his or her residence within 30 days of service of a written request for those documents. Those documents shall also be provided to the homeowner in conjunction with the initial sale of the residence.

(c) At the expense of the homeowner, who may opt to use an offsite copy facility that is bonded and insured, a builder shall provide to the homeowner or his or her legal representative copies of all manufactured products maintenance, preventive maintenance, and limited warranty information within 30 days of a written request for those documents. These documents shall also be provided to the homeowner in conjunction with the initial sale of the residence.

(d) At the expense of the homeowner, who may opt to use an offsite copy facility that is bonded and insured, a builder shall provide to the homeowner or his or her legal representative copies of all of the builder's limited contractual warranties in accordance with this part in effect at the time of the original sale of the residence within 30 days of a written request for those documents. Those documents shall also be provided to the homeowner in conjunction with the initial sale of the residence.

(e) A builder shall maintain the name and address of an agent for notice pursuant to this chapter with the Secretary of State or, alternatively, elect to use a third party for that notice if the builder has notified the homeowner in writing of the third party's name and address, to whom claims and requests for information under this section may be mailed. The name and address of the agent for notice or third party shall be included with the original sales documentation and shall be initialed and acknowledged by the purchaser and the builder's sales representative.

This subdivision applies to instances in which a builder contracts with a third party to accept claims and act on the builder's behalf. A builder shall give actual notice to the homeowner that the builder has made such an election, and shall include the name and address of the third party.

(f) A builder shall record on title a notice of the existence of these procedures and a notice that these procedures impact the legal rights of the homeowner. This information shall also be included with the original sales documentation and shall be initialed and acknowledged by the purchaser and the builder's sales representative.

(g) A builder shall provide, with the original sales documentation, a written copy of this title, which shall be initialed and acknowledged by the purchaser and the builder's sales representative.

(h) As to any documents provided in conjunction with the original sale, the builder shall instruct the original purchaser to provide those documents to any subsequent purchaser.

(i) Any builder who fails to comply with any of these requirements within the time specified is not entitled to the protection of this chapter, and the homeowner is released from the requirements of this chapter and may proceed with the filing of an action, in which case the remaining chapters of this part shall continue to apply to the action.

## § 913. Written acknowledgement of claim; time to respond; contents

A builder or his or her representative shall acknowledge, in writing, receipt of the notice of the claim within 14 days after receipt of the notice of the claim. If the notice of the claim is served by the claimant's legal representative, or if the builder receives a written representation letter from a homeowner's attorney, the builder shall include the attorney in all subsequent substantive communications, including, without limitation, all written communications occurring pursuant to this chapter, and all substantive and procedural communications, including all written communications, following the commencement of any subsequent complaint or other legal action, except that if the builder has retained or involved legal counsel to assist the builder in this process, all communications by the builder's counsel shall only be with the claimant's legal representative, if any.

## § 914. Election to pursue other nonadversarial contractual procedures; affect of Title 7 upon exiting statutory or decisional law

(a) This chapter establishes a nonadversarial procedure, including the remedies available under this chapter which, if the procedure does not resolve the dispute between the parties, may result in a subsequent action to enforce the other chapters of this title. A builder may attempt to commence nonadversarial contractual provisions other than the nonadversarial procedures and remedies set forth in this chapter, but may not, in addition to its own nonadversarial contractual provisions, require adherence to the nonadversarial procedures and remedies set forth in this chapter, regardless of whether the builder's own alternative nonadversarial contractual provisions are successful in resolving the dispute or ultimately deemed enforceable.

At the time the sales agreement is executed, the builder shall notify the homeowner whether the builder intends to engage in the nonadversarial procedure of this section or attempt to enforce alternative nonadversarial contractual provisions. If the builder elects to use alternative nonadversarial contractual provisions in lieu of this chapter, the election is binding, regardless of whether the builder's alternative nonadversarial contractual provisions are successful in resolving the ultimate dispute or are ultimately deemed enforceable.

(b) Nothing in this title is intended to affect existing statutory or decisional law pertaining to the applicability, viability, or enforceability of alternative dispute resolution methods, alternative remedies, or contractual arbitration, judicial reference, or similar procedures requiring a binding resolution to enforce the other chapters of this title or any other disputes between homeowners and builders. Nothing in this title is intended to affect the applicability, viability, or enforceability, if any, of contractual arbitration or judicial reference after a nonadversarial procedure or provision has been completed.

## § 915. Application of prelitigation provisions upon certain failures to act by builder

If a builder fails to acknowledge receipt of the notice of a claim within the time specified, elects not to go through the process set forth in this chapter, or fails to request an inspection within the time specified, or at the conclusion or cessation of an alternative nonadversarial proceeding, this chapter does not apply and the homeowner is released from the requirements of this chapter and may proceed with the filing of an action. However, the standards set forth in the other chapters of this title shall continue to apply to the action.

## § 916. Builder election to inspect

(a) If a builder elects to inspect the claimed unmet standards, the builder shall complete the initial inspection and testing within 14 days after acknowledgment of receipt of the notice of the claim, at a mutually convenient date and time. If the homeowner has retained legal representation, the inspection shall be scheduled with the legal representative's office at a mutually convenient date and time, unless the legal representative is unavailable during the relevant time periods. All costs of builder inspection and testing, including any damage caused by the builder inspection, shall be borne by the builder. The builder shall also provide written proof that the builder has liability insurance to cover any damages or injuries occurring during inspection and testing. The builder shall restore the property to its pretesting condition within 48 hours of the testing. The builder shall, upon request, allow the inspections to be observed and electronically recorded, video recorded, or photographed by the claimant or his or her legal representative.

(b) Nothing that occurs during a builder's or claimant's inspection or testing may be used or introduced as evidence to support a spoliation defense by any potential party in any subsequent litigation.

(c) If a builder deems a second inspection or testing reasonably necessary, and specifies the reasons therefor in writing within three days following the initial inspection, the builder may conduct a second inspection or testing. A second inspection or testing shall be completed within 40 days of the initial inspection or testing. All requirements concerning the initial inspection or testing shall also apply to the second inspection or testing.

(d) If the builder fails to inspect or test the property within the time specified, the claimant is released from the requirements of this section and may proceed with the filing of an action. However, the standards set forth in the other chapters of this title shall continue to apply to the action.

(e) If a builder intends to hold a subcontractor, design professional, individual product manufacturer, or material supplier, including an insurance carrier, warranty company, or service company, responsible for its contribution to the unmet standard, the builder shall provide notice to that person or entity sufficiently in advance to allow them to attend the initial, or if requested, second inspection of any alleged unmet standard and to participate in the repair process. The claimant and his or her legal representative, if any, shall be advised in a reasonable time prior to the inspection as to the identity of all persons or entities invited to attend. This subdivision does not apply to the builder's insurance company. Except with respect to any claims involving a repair actually conducted under this chapter, nothing in this subdivision shall be construed to relieve a subcontractor, design professional, individual product manufacturer, or material supplier of any liability under an action brought by a claimant.

## § 917. Written offer to repair

Within 30 days of the initial or, if requested, second inspection or testing, the builder may offer in writing to repair the violation. The offer to repair shall also compensate the homeowner for all applicable damages recoverable under Section 944, within the timeframe for the repair set forth in this chapter. Any such offer shall be accompanied by a detailed, specific, step-by-step statement identifying the particular violation that is being repaired, explaining the nature, scope, and location of the repair, and setting a reasonable completion date for the repair. The offer shall also include the names, addresses, telephone numbers, and license numbers of the contractors whom the builder intends to have perform the repair. Those contractors shall be fully insured for, and shall be responsible for, all damages or injuries that they may cause to occur during the repair, and evidence of that insurance shall be provided to the homeowner upon request. Upon written request by the homeowner or his or her legal representative, and within the timeframes set forth in this chapter, the builder shall also provide any available technical documentation, including, without limitation, plans and specifications, pertaining to the claimed violation within the particular home or development tract. The offer shall also advise the homeowner in writing of his or her right to request up to three additional contractors from which to select to do the repair pursuant to this chapter.

### § 918. Homeowner response to repair offer

Upon receipt of the offer to repair, the homeowner shall have 30 days to authorize the builder to proceed with the repair. The homeowner may alternatively request, at the homeowner's sole option and discretion, that the builder provide the names, addresses, telephone numbers, and license numbers for up to three alternative contractors who are not owned or financially controlled by the builder and who regularly conduct business in the county where the structure is located. If the homeowner so elects, the builder is entitled to an additional noninvasive inspection, to occur at a mutually convenient date and time within 20 days of the election, so as to permit the other proposed contractors to review the proposed site of the repair. Within 35 days after the request of the homeowner for alternative contractors, the builder shall present the homeowner with a choice of contractors. Within 20 days after that presentation, the homeowner shall authorize the builder or one of the alternative contractors to perform the repair.

### § 919. Mediation by mutual agreement; unresolved disputes; repairs

The offer to repair shall also be accompanied by an offer to mediate the dispute if the homeowner so chooses. The mediation shall be limited to a four-hour mediation, except as otherwise mutually agreed before a nonaffiliated mediator selected and paid for by the builder. At the homeowner's sole option, the homeowner may agree to split the cost of the mediator, and if he or she does so, the mediator shall be selected jointly. The mediator shall have sufficient availability such that the mediation occurs within 15 days after the request to mediate is received and occurs at a mutually convenient location within the county where the action is pending. If a builder has made an offer to repair a violation, and the mediation has failed to resolve the dispute, the homeowner shall allow the repair to be performed either by the builder, its contractor, or the selected contractor.

### § 920. Claimant right to file action

If the builder fails to make an offer to repair or otherwise strictly comply with this chapter within the times specified, the claimant is released from the requirements of this chapter and may proceed with the filing of an action. If the contractor performing the repair does not complete the repair in the time or manner specified, the claimant may file an action. If this occurs, the standards set forth in the other chapters of this part shall continue to apply to the action.

### § 921. Repair work; time and date scheduled; completion date

(a) In the event that a resolution under this chapter involves a repair by the builder, the builder shall make an appointment with the claimant, make all appropriate arrangements to effectuate a repair of the claimed unmet standards, and compensate the homeowner for all damages resulting therefrom free of charge to the claimant. The repair shall be scheduled through the claimant's legal representative, if any, unless he or she is unavailable during the relevant time periods. The repair shall be commenced on a mutually convenient date within 14 days of acceptance or, if an alternative contractor is selected by the homeowner, within 14 days of the selection, or, if a mediation occurs, within seven days of the mediation, or within five days after a permit is obtained if one is required. The builder shall act with reasonable diligence in obtaining any such permit.

(b) The builder shall ensure that work done on the repairs is done with the utmost diligence, and that the repairs are completed as soon as reasonably possible, subject to the nature of the repair or some unforeseen event not caused by the builder or the contractor performing the repair. Every effort shall be made to complete the repair within 120 days.

### § 922. Electronic recordation, video recordation, or photographs during repair work

The builder shall, upon request, allow the repair to be observed and electronically recorded, video recorded, or photographed by the claimant or his or her legal representative. Nothing that occurs during the repair process may be used or introduced as evidence to support a spoliation defense by any potential party in any subsequent litigation.

### § 923. Documentation relating to repair work; requests for copies

The builder shall provide the homeowner or his or her legal representative, upon request, with copies of all correspondence, photographs, and other materials pertaining or relating in any manner to the repairs.

### § 924. Partial repair of claims; statement of reasons

If the builder elects to repair some, but not all of, the claimed unmet standards, the builder shall, at the same time it makes its offer, set forth with particularity in writing the reasons, and the support for those reasons, for not repairing all claimed unmet standards.

### § 925. Failure to repair within time allowed

If the builder fails to complete the repair within the time specified in the repair plan, the claimant is released from the requirements of this chapter and may proceed with the filing of an action. If this occurs, the standards set forth in the other chapters of this title shall continue to apply to the action.

## § 926. Release or waiver in exchange for repair work

The builder may not obtain a release or waiver of any kind in exchange for the repair work mandated by this chapter. At the conclusion of the repair, the claimant may proceed with filing an action for violation of the applicable standard or for a claim of inadequate repair, or both, including all applicable damages available under Section 944.

## § 927. Claims for violation of statutory process or inadequate repair; limitation of action; extension of time

If the applicable statute of limitations has otherwise run during this process, the time period for filing a complaint or other legal remedies for violation of any provision of this title, or for a claim of inadequate repair, is extended from the time of the original claim by the claimant to 100 days after the repair is completed, whether or not the particular violation is the one being repaired. If the builder fails to acknowledge the claim within the time specified, elects not to go through this statutory process, or fails to request an inspection within the time specified, the time period for filing a complaint or other legal remedies for violation of any provision of this title is extended from the time of the original claim by the claimant to 45 days after the time for responding to the notice of claim has expired. If the builder elects to attempt to enforce its own nonadversarial procedure in lieu of the procedure set forth in this chapter, the time period for filing a complaint or other legal remedies for violation of any provision of this part is extended from the time of the original claim by the claimant to 100 days after either the completion of the builder's alternative nonadversarial procedure, or 100 days after the builder's alternative nonadversarial procedure is deemed unenforceable, whichever is later.

## § 928. Mediation after repair completion

If the builder has invoked this chapter and completed a repair, prior to filing an action, if there has been no previous mediation between the parties, the homeowner or his or her legal representative shall request mediation in writing. The mediation shall be limited to four hours, except as otherwise mutually agreed before a nonaffiliated mediator selected and paid for by the builder. At the homeowner's sole option, the homeowner may agree to split the cost of the mediator and if he or she does so, the mediator shall be selected jointly. The mediator shall have sufficient availability such that the mediation will occur within 15 days after the request for mediation is received and shall occur at a mutually convenient location within the county where the action is pending. In the event that a mediation is used at this point, any applicable statutes of limitations shall be tolled from the date of the request to mediate until the next court day after the mediation is completed, or the 100-day period, whichever is later.

## § 929. Cash offer in lieu of repair; release

(a) Nothing in this chapter prohibits the builder from making only a cash offer and no repair. In this situation, the homeowner is free to accept the offer, or he or she may reject the offer and proceed with the filing of an action. If the latter occurs, the standards of the other chapters of this title shall continue to apply to the action.

(b) The builder may obtain a reasonable release in exchange for the cash payment. The builder may negotiate the terms and conditions of any reasonable release in terms of scope and consideration in conjunction with a cash payment under this chapter.

## § 930. Failure to act within mandated timeframes and other requirements; right to file action; motion to stay proceedings

(a) The time periods and all other requirements in this chapter are to be strictly construed, and, unless extended by the mutual agreement of the parties in accordance with this chapter, shall govern the rights and obligations under this title. If a builder fails to act in accordance with this section within the timeframes mandated, unless extended by the mutual agreement of the parties as evidenced by a postclaim written confirmation by the affected homeowner demonstrating that he or she has knowingly and voluntarily extended the statutory timeframe, the claimant may proceed with filing an action. If this occurs, the standards of the other chapters of this title shall continue to apply to the action.

(b) If the claimant does not conform with the requirements of this chapter, the builder may bring a motion to stay any subsequent court action or other proceeding until the requirements of this chapter have been satisfied. The court, in its discretion, may award the prevailing party on such a motion, his or her attorney's fees and costs in bringing or opposing the motion.

## § 931. Causes of action or damages exceeding scope of actionable defects; applicability of standards

If a claim combines causes of action or damages not covered by this part, including, without limitation, personal injuries, class actions, other statutory remedies, or fraud-based claims, the claimed unmet standards shall be administered according to this part, although evidence of the property in its unrepaired condition may be introduced to support the respective elements of any such cause of action. As to any fraud-based claim, if the fact that the property has been repaired under this chapter is deemed admissible, the trier of fact shall be informed that the repair was not voluntarily accepted by the homeowner. As to any class action claims that address solely the incorporation of a defective component into a residence, the named and unnamed class members need not comply with this chapter.

## § 932. Subsequently discovered claims of unmet standards

Subsequently discovered claims of unmet standards shall be administered separately under this chapter, unless otherwise agreed to by the parties. However, in the case of a detached single family residence, in the same home, if the subsequently discovered claim is for a violation of the same standard as that which has already been initiated by the same claimant and the subject of a currently pending action, the claimant need not reinitiate the process as to the same standard. In the case of an attached project, if the subsequently discovered claim is for a violation of the same standard for a connected component system in the same building as has already been initiated by the same claimant, and the subject of a currently pending action, the claimant need not reinitiate this process as to that standard.

## § 933. Evidence of repair efforts

If any enforcement of these standards is commenced, the fact that a repair effort was made may be introduced to the trier of fact. However, the claimant may use the condition of the property prior to the repair as the basis for contending that the repair work was inappropriate, inadequate, or incomplete, or that the violation still exists. The claimant need not show that the repair work resulted in further damage nor that damage has continued to occur as a result of the violation.

## § 934. Evidence of conduct during enforcement process

Evidence of both parties' conduct during this process may be introduced during a subsequent enforcement action, if any, with the exception of any mediation. Any repair efforts undertaken by the builder, shall not be considered settlement communications or offers of settlement and are not inadmissible in evidence on such a basis.

## § 935. Construction of chapter with similar provisions

To the extent that provisions of this chapter are enforced and those provisions are substantially similar to provisions in Section 6000, but an action is subsequently commenced under Section 6000, the parties are excused from performing the substantially similar requirements under Section 6000.

## § 936. Parties subject to application of title; determination; defenses available; joint and several liability; strict liability

Each and every provision of the other chapters of this title apply to general contractors, subcontractors, material suppliers, individual product manufacturers, and design professionals to the extent that the general contractors, subcontractors, material suppliers, individual product manufacturers, and design professionals caused, in whole or in part, a violation of a particular standard as the result of a negligent act or omission or a breach of contract. In addition to the affirmative defenses set forth in Section 945.5, a general contractor, subcontractor, material supplier, design professional, individual product manufacturer, or other entity may also offer common law and contractual defenses as applicable to any claimed violation of a standard. All actions by a claimant or builder to enforce an express contract, or any provision thereof, against a general contractor, subcontractor, material supplier, individual product manufacturer, or design professional is preserved. Nothing in this title modifies the law pertaining to joint and several liability for builders, general contractors, subcontractors, material suppliers, individual product manufacturer, and design professionals that contribute to any specific violation of this title. However, the negligence standard in this section does not apply to any general contractor, subcontractor, material supplier, individual product manufacturer, or design professional with respect to claims for which strict liability would apply.

### § 937. Construction with professional negligence actions

Nothing in this title shall be interpreted to eliminate or abrogate the requirement to comply with Section 411.35 of the Code of Civil Procedure or to affect the liability of design professionals, including architects and architectural firms, for claims and damages not covered by this title.

### § 938. Application of Title 7 to certain residences

This title applies only to new residential units where the purchase agreement with the buyer was signed by the seller on or after January 1, 2003.


## Chapter 5 – Procedure

### § 941. Limitation of action; tolling

(a) Except as specifically set forth in this title, no action may be brought to recover under this title more than 10 years after substantial completion of the improvement but not later than the date of recordation of a valid notice of completion.

(b) As used in this section, "action" includes an action for indemnity brought against a person arising out of that person's performance or furnishing of services or materials referred to in this title, except that a cross-complaint for indemnity may be filed pursuant to subdivision (b) of Section 428.10 of the Code of Civil Procedure in an action which has been brought within the time period set forth in subdivision (a).

(c) The limitation prescribed by this section may not be asserted by way of defense by any person in actual possession or the control, as owner, tenant or otherwise, of such an improvement, at the time any deficiency in the improvement constitutes the proximate cause for which it is proposed to make a claim or bring an action.

(d) Sections 337.15 and 337.1 of the Code of Civil Procedure do not apply to actions under this title.

(e) Existing statutory and decisional law regarding tolling of the statute of limitations shall apply to the time periods for filing an action or making a claim under this title, except that repairs made pursuant to Chapter 4 (commencing with Section 910), with the exception of the tolling provision contained in Section 927, do not extend the period for filing an action, or restart the time limitations contained in subdivision (a) or (b) of Section 7091 of the Business and Professions Code. If a builder arranges for a contractor to perform a repair pursuant to Chapter 4 (commencing with Section 910), as to the builder the time period for calculating the statute of limitation in subdivision (a) or (b) of Section 7091 of the Business and Professions Code shall pertain to the substantial completion of the original construction and not to the date of repairs under this title. The time limitations established by this title do not apply to any action by a claimant for a contract or express contractual provision. Causes of action and damages to which this chapter does not apply are not limited by this section.

## § 942. Sufficiency of claim for violation of Chapter 2 standards

In order to make a claim for violation of the standards set forth in Chapter 2 (commencing with Section 896), a homeowner need only demonstrate, in accordance with the applicable evidentiary standard, that the home does not meet the applicable standard, subject to the affirmative defenses set forth in Section 945.5. No further showing of causation or damages is required to meet the burden of proof regarding a violation of a standard set forth in Chapter 2 (commencing with Section 896), provided that the violation arises out of, pertains to, or is related to, the original construction.

## § 943. Exclusiveness of title; exceptions

(a) Except as provided in this title, no other cause of action for a claim covered by this title or for damages recoverable under Section 944 is allowed. In addition to the rights under this title, this title does not apply to any action by a claimant to enforce a contract or express contractual provision, or any action for fraud, personal injury, or violation of a statute. Damages awarded for the items set forth in Section 944 in such other cause of action shall be reduced by the amounts recovered pursuant to Section 944 for violation of the standards set forth in this title.

(b) As to any claims involving a detached single-family home, the homeowner's right to the reasonable value of repairing any nonconformity is limited to the repair costs, or the diminution in current value of the home caused by the nonconformity, whichever is less, subject to the personal use exception as developed under common law.

## § 944. Damages; determination of amount

If a claim for damages is made under this title, the homeowner is only entitled to damages for the reasonable value of repairing any violation of the standards set forth in this title, the reasonable cost of repairing any damages caused by the repair efforts, the reasonable cost of repairing and rectifying any damages resulting from the failure of the home to meet the standards, the reasonable cost of removing and replacing any improper repair by the builder, reasonable relocation and storage expenses, lost business income if the home was used as a principal place of a business licensed to be operated from the home, reasonable investigative costs for each established violation, and all other costs or fees recoverable by contract or statute.

## § 945. Binding effect upon original purchasers and their successors-in-interest

The provisions, standards, rights, and obligations set forth in this title are binding upon all original purchasers and their successors-in-interest. For purposes of this title, associations and others having the rights set forth in Sections 4810 and 4815 shall be considered to be original purchasers and shall have standing to enforce the provisions, standards, rights, and obligations set forth in this title.

## § 945.5. Affirmative defenses

A builder, general contractor, subcontractor, material supplier, individual product manufacturer, or design professional, under the principles of comparative fault pertaining to affirmative defenses, may be excused, in whole or in part, from any obligation, damage, loss, or liability if the builder, general contractor, subcontractor, material supplier, individual product manufacturer, or design professional, can demonstrate any of the following affirmative defenses in response to a claimed violation:

(a) To the extent it is caused by an unforeseen act of nature which caused the structure not to meet the standard. For purposes of this section an "unforeseen act of nature" means a weather condition, earthquake, or manmade event such as war, terrorism, or vandalism, in excess of the design criteria expressed by the applicable building codes, regulations, and ordinances in effect at the time of original construction.

(b) To the extent it is caused by a homeowner's unreasonable failure to minimize or prevent those damages in a timely manner, including the failure of the homeowner to allow reasonable and timely access for inspections and repairs under this title. This includes the failure to give timely notice to the builder after discovery of a violation, but does not include damages due to the untimely or inadequate response of a builder to the homeowner's claim.

(c) To the extent it is caused by the homeowner or his or her agent, employee, general contractor, subcontractor, independent contractor, or consultant by virtue of their failure to follow the builder's or manufacturer's recommendations, or commonly accepted homeowner maintenance obligations. In order to rely upon this defense as it relates to a builder's recommended maintenance schedule, the builder shall show that the homeowner had written notice of these schedules and recommendations and that the recommendations and schedules were reasonable at the time they were issued.

(d) To the extent it is caused by the homeowner or his or her agent's or an independent third party's alterations, ordinary wear and tear, misuse, abuse, or neglect, or by the structure's use for something other than its intended purpose.

(e) To the extent that the time period for filing actions bars the claimed violation.

(f) As to a particular violation for which the builder has obtained a valid release.

(g) To the extent that the builder's repair was successful in correcting the particular violation of the applicable standard.

(h) As to any causes of action to which this statute does not apply, all applicable affirmative defenses are preserved.

# Chapter 5

# SB 800 Cases

SB800 or Civil Code §895 et seq. is a relatively new statute. It went into effect on January 1, 2003 for homes first sold on or after January 1, 2003. Thus, in order for the statute to have applied to a lawsuit, the home must have been sold on or after this date.

For a "published" case to exist, the following must have occurred:

1. A home must be built and then sold on or after January 1, 2003.
2. A homeowner or an Association must then make a claim under the statute and give the builder a "Right to Repair."
3. A Homeowner Association must comply with the remaining time in the "Calderon" process before filing suit.
4. A Homeowner and/or an Association must file a lawsuit.
5. The Lawsuit must have a ruling (during the case or after a trial) that is subject to review by the Court of Appeal.
6. The Court of Appeal must take the Writ (a writ is an "appeal" during the case).
7. The case must go to trial and then a verdict reached.
8. Then, someone must make the decision to file an Appeal – the losing party.
9. The case is briefed for the Court of Appeal.
10. A decision is written and published.

Because the statute is relatively young, there are not a lot of cases that have been published. This chapter will discuss the cases that have been published to date.

# Exclusive Remedy?

SB800; Strict Liability; and Negligence – Is SB800 an Exclusive Remedy or Does a Homeowner/Association have the right to plead recovery under all three theories?

Civil Code §896 provides that a builder and its subcontractors shall be liable for violation of the standards set forth in the statute, except as set forth in the Title (Statute). What does this mean?

### *Liberty Mutual Insurance Company v. Brookfield Crystal Cove, LLC (2013) 219 Cal. App. 4th 98*

This case held that SB800 was not an exclusive remedy. It opened the doors to allow homeowners and Associations to file suit for violations of the Standards set forth in SB800, Strict Liability and Negligence.

Following this decision, many homeowners and Associations began amending their complaints to add causes of action for strict liability and negligence.

When negotiating the statute, the intent was to *replace* strict liability and negligence (common law rules) with SB800 (a statutory rule). Common law means that it is Court or Judge made law. Statutory rule means that the legislature passed a bill and the governor signed it into law. The statute has some exceptions and allows for claims outside the statute in some situations.

### *Burch v. Superior Court (2014) 223 Cal. App. 4th 1411*

This case held in line with the Liberty Mutual case. It too found that homeowners and Associations can bring common law actions in addition to violations of the statutory violations.

### *McMillan Albany LLC v. Superior Court (2015) 239 Cal. App. 4th 1132*

In this case, the plaintiff Homeowners filed suit alleging both statutory violations and common law claims for strict liability and negligence. The developer argued that it still had the statutory right to repair and the Court of Appeal agreed.

The McMillan court also disagreed with the Liberty Mutual court. The McMillan court held that SB800 was an exclusive remedy and that the homeowners did not have the right to pursue Strict Liability and/or Negligence claims.

This decision is now before the California Supreme Court. Review was granted at 360 P. 3d 1022.

# The Right to Repair – Failure to Give Notice

The first cases that came down concerned whether or not the homeowner/association or the builder had to "prove" that the right to repair applied or did not apply to a particular home/association. The statute requires that a builder who wants to retain the right to repair, must provide the purchasing homeowner with specific items. In addition, the builder must record a notice of the statute in the title for the home. There are many other requirements but the first cases challenged whether or not the homeowner had to prove that the builder failed to comply or whether the builder had to prove that it had complied.

### Standard Pacific Corporation v. Superior Court (2009) 176 Cal. App. 4<sup>th</sup> 828

In this case, the homeowners brought an action against a builder for common law claims (strict liability, negligence, etc) and tried to avoid the pre-litigation right to repair by the builder. The builder moved to stay the lawsuit so that it would have the opportunity to make repairs. The Court of Appeal agreed and held that the homeowners, not the builder, must prove that the right to repair has been voided or is not applicable to a particular case.

### Baeza v. Superior Court (2011) 201 Cal. App. 4<sup>th</sup> 1214

In this case, the builder "opted out" or attempted to insert its own pre-litigation procedure into place instead of the procedure set forth in SB800. The statute provides that the builder gets the statutory pre-litigation right to repair or it can opt out and insert its own procedure. This procedure though cannot be more burdensome on the homeowner than the statutory right. Thus, a builder can be more generous in the pre-litigation procedure toward the homeowner, not toward itself.

In this case the homeowners challenged the builder's pre-litigation procedure and argued that it was in violation of the statute. This in turn voided the "right to repair" under the statute.

The homeowners used a document request to void the builder's right to its pre-litigation procedure. The Court of Appeal held that the document request did not apply because the builder opted out of the statutory right to repair.

### *KB Home Greater Los Angeles, Inc. v. Superior Court (2014) 223 Cal. App. 4th 1471*

In this case, an insurance company, after making repairs for its insured, sued the builder for violations of the standards set forth in SB800. The builder argued that it was not given its right to repair and thus the standards did not apply. The Court of Appeal agreed.

This decision is important to note as homeowners who become aware of problems or violations of standards should first give a builder the right to repair under the statute. The timelines under the statute are short. Failure to provide the opportunity could void your right to recover.

If your home is flooding you should still work to stop the damage from spreading. If at all possible, give notice. If not, make as little of the repair as possible to allow the builder to finish the repair.

### *McMillin Albany LLC v. Superior Court (2015) 239 Cal. App. 4th 1132*

In this case, homeowners brought an action against the builder and attempted to avoid the pre-litigation right to repair. The homeowners alleged common law causes of action instead of the statutory violations. The builder sought to enforce its rights to first make repairs. The Court of Appeal agreed with the builder and held that homeowners must first provide a builder with the opportunity to make repairs under the statute before filing a lawsuit.

# Alternative Pre-Litigation Procedure Voids Statutory Pre-Litigation Requirements

### *Anders v. Superior Court (2011) 192 Cal. App. 4th 579*

In this case the homeowners brought an action against a builder without following the builder's pre-litigation procedure. The homeowners argued that the pre-litigation procedure was void under the statute. The trial court and Court of Appeal agreed.

The Court of Appeal found that the builder's attempt to enforce a pre-litigation procedure that was not enforceable voided the builder's rights to such a procedure under the statute. The Court of Appeal also found that the builder's attempts to hold subsequent purchasers to the contractual pre-litigation procedures also voided the builder's rights to the statutory procedures against them.

### *McCaffrey Group, Inc. v. Superior Court (2014) 224 Cal. App. 4th 1330*

In this case, the builder opted out of SB800's pre-litigation process. Instead, it inserted its own procedures for homeowners to follow. The homeowners filed suit and the builder moved to compel compliance with its pre-litigation procedure. The trial court denied the motion of the builder. The Court of Appeal however, agreed with the builder's argument.

It should be noted that each builder "alternative" pre-litigation procedure will need to be judged on its specific facts. This case may open the door for builders to enforce their own pre-litigation procedures but it may not as the type of procedure implemented is fact specific.

Builders should avoid trying to make the pre-litigation process take longer or make it more complicated. The spirit of the statute is to provide a quick and simple remedy to homeowners. It is not designed to be replaced with a long drawn out process that makes it more difficult for homeowners to have their homes fixed.

# Request for Documents – Before or After a Notice of Claim?

*Darling v. Superior Court (2012) 211 Cal. App. 4th 69*

In this case, the homeowners made a pre-notice of claim request for documents. The builder declined to provide the documents and argued that it did not have to do so until after a Notice of Claim was sent by the homeowners. The trial court and Court of Appeal agreed. Thus, according to this decision, a document request can be sent with a Notice of Claim or after a Notice of Claim has been sent to the builder.

The statute provides for the document request so that a Notice of Claim can be prepared using the plans and specifications. Without the plans and specifications along with this decision, a Notice of Claim is not required to be as specific as many builders are demanding.

# Release for Money Instead of Repairs

One of the protections under the statute for homeowners and associations is that a builder cannot obtain a release for the payment of money unless it is reasonable. In addition, when a builder makes repairs, it cannot do so in exchange for a release. (Civil Code §926)

**Belasco v. Wells (2015) 234 Cal. App. 409**

In this case, a homeowner received $25,000 in exchange for a release from a builder under the statute. The homeowner took the money and then filed a lawsuit. The homeowner argued that the provisions of the statute do not allow for a release. The trial court and the Court of Appeal disagreed.

The Court found that the homeowner, an attorney, knowingly accepted the money in exchange for a release. The court did not find any fraud to void the release and upheld the release.

The lesson to be learned is that if you sign a release it may be enforceable. The statute is designed to protect homeowners from unwittingly signing a release for their entire home if they are paid for one item. For example, before SB800 was enacted, builders would offer a homeowner $500 for their door and get a general release for the entire house. This is unreasonable. The statute makes this unenforceable but it does allow for the payment of money in exchange for a release if it is reasonable.

# Economic Loss – Indemnity – Burden of Proof

### *Greystone Homes, Inc. v. Midtec (2008) 168 Cal. App. 4th 1194*

One of the most complicated cases to come down from the Court of Appeal comes from a case that involved a builder who made repairs for its homeowners. The builder then pursued the subcontractor and material suppliers for the defective products it provided during construction. Under the statute, this is exactly what a builder who cares about its customers should do.

Here that is what the builder did but the Court of Appeal made it more difficult for the builder to recover from its subcontractors and its material suppliers. This decision makes builders more likely to want to resolve an entire case with cooperation from its subcontractors rather than make repairs and seek compensation later.

This decision discussed other issues as well. Some of which are not rules but are often cited by counsel seeking to persuade a trial court. For example, the decision counters the express language of Civil Code §936 when it comes to material suppliers. The decision seems to suggest that a "negligence" standard applies.

Fortunately, from a homeowner or Association standpoint, there was no representation in this case and thus the decision should not apply to homeowners or Associations. The clear language of Civil Code §936 should prevail. When read in conjunction with *Jiminez v. Superior Court*, a manufacturer who is subject to strict liability under the common law, the builder's no-fault standard should apply. Some courts hold that a homeowner or an Association must show that the violation of the standard was caused in whole or in part by the material supplier/manufacturer.

The decision clearly supports the fact that the statute reverses the California Supreme Court decision in *Aas v. Superior Court (2000) 24 Cal. 4th 627*. In the *Aas* decision, the Court held that unless a defect causes damage as opposed to solely an economic loss (damage to the particular product itself), a homeowner cannot recover for the defective condition. The Court in *Greystone* held that the Legislature, taking its cue from the California Supreme Court in the *Aas* decision, reversed that when it enacted SB800.

SB800 has several standards that do not require damage to be proven. It sets forth standards that if violated are subject to the recovery of money or a builder's repair if done in conjunction with the pre-litigation process.

# Chapter 6

# Homeowner Association Specific Issues and Requirements

If you are a Homeowners Association, there are often special requirements that you must follow before bringing a construction defect claim. In addition, there are special requirements that must be followed both during and at the conclusion of construction defect cases. This chapter will discuss those special requirements.

### Standing – Who Can File a Claim?

§ 5980. Standing

An association has standing to institute, defend, settle, or intervene in litigation, arbitration, mediation, or administrative proceedings in its own name as the real party in interest and without joining with it the members, in matters pertaining to the following:

(a) Enforcement of the governing documents.

(b) Damage to the common area.

(c) Damage to a separate interest that the association is obligated to maintain or repair.

(d) Damage to a separate interest that arises out of, or is integrally related to, damage to the common area or a separate interest that the association is obligated to maintain or repair.

The first issue is to determine whether or not the defect or standard violation is located in the common area or a separate interest area. In order to answer this question, you must look at the Association's Governing Documents. Generally, the answer is located in the CC&Rs.

It is important to remember that if a separate interest is being damaged because of a common area defect or standard violation, the Association will have standing under Civil Code §5980(d).

Sometimes the answer is not clear. There are other ways around the issue of standing. They include the following:

1. Assignment of Rights
2. Amending the CC&Rs
3. File a Representative Action
4. Certify the Action as a Class Action

Each of the above ways around the issue of standing have their own issues and complications. Getting an Assignment of Rights will require the preparation of an Assignment Agreement. The Agreement will need to be signed by the member/owner and the Association. This will need to be done for each unit/home. Those that do not sign an Assignment Agreement will not have assigned their rights and they will retain their rights. The homeowner in that situation would need to bring their own action against the builder.

Amending the CC&Rs can also be complicated. In addition, many CC&Rs have limitations of when certain provisions that relate to construction defects and/or standing can be amended. Builders have placed these limits to make bringing construction defect claims more difficult and/or complicated. Before the *Pinnacle* decision, this type of provision could be ignored. Following the decision in *Pinnacle* – although an Arbitration decision – the issue is more complicated.

The California Supreme Court held that a Federal Arbitration Act arbitration clause in an Association's CC&Rs is enforceable against the Association and its members. The logical and possible extension could be that other provisions that "protect" builders too could be enforceable. The decision to argue that such a provision is or is not enforceable is complicated and will require consultation with an attorney who handles construction defect cases.

**What is the Statute of Limitations and when does it start to run?**

One of the most important questions that must be answered is whether or not a claim can be made. In other words – has the statute of limitations run or do you have more time? This question seems simple but it can become complicated.

Under the common law the time when the statute of limitations began to run was measured by the filing of a Notice of Completion. A document that was filed with the County Recorder told us when the 10-year statute of limitations would run. Under SB800, the time for when the statute of limitations begins to run is from the original close of escrow. However, for an Association, the definition is different.

### § 895. Definitions

(e) "Close of escrow" means the date of the close of escrow between the builder and the original homeowner. With respect to claims by an association, as defined in Section 4080, "close of escrow" means the date of substantial completion, as defined in Section 337.15 of the Code of Civil Procedure, or the date the builder relinquishes control over the association's ability to decide whether to initiate a claim under this title, whichever is later.

The statute provides that if a builder controls the board of directors' ability to initiate a claim the time does not start to run against an Association's ability to bring a claim. When the statute was written it was common for builders to stay on boards of directors while a project was being completed. Sometimes builders would stay on longer. The problem was that if a builder dominated and/or controlled a board, it could effectively take away the Association's ability to pursue a claim for violations of SB800.

Out of a concern that builders would simply stay on the Board for 10 years, the statute provides that if the builder has control over the Association's ability to decide whether or not to initiate a claim, the clock does not start to run.

Another problem has emerged since the writing of SB800. That is builders who have written into the CC&Rs a provision that states that when the first homeowner is elected or placed on the Board of Directors, that homeowner has the ability on their own to initiate a claim under SB800. The reality is that the homeowner often does not understand this ability as they look at the board and see 1 vote verses 4 builder seats.

This issue has not been determined by any Courts of Appeal but it is likely to present itself in the future. If you have an Association that is close to 10 years old, you should not wait and bank on this provision protecting you. If you have passed the time and need to invoke this argument, you should do so but you need to be aware of the counter arguments that will be made.

## The Calderon Act

Included in the Davis-Sterling Act is a provision often referred to as the Calderon Act. Essentially, this Act provides for a version of a pre-litigation process that will run concurrently with an SB800 pre-litigation procedure. The difference is that the Calderon Act pre-litigation procedure is longer – it goes 180 days and can be extended by stipulation for another 180 days.

The Calderon Act includes many requirements that both the Association and Declarant must follow.

**§ 6000. Actions for damages against common interest development builders, developers, or general contractors**

(a) Before an association files a complaint for damages against a builder, developer, or general contractor (respondent) of a common interest development based upon a claim for defects in the design or construction of the common interest development, all of the requirements of this section shall be satisfied with respect to the builder, developer, or general contractor.

(b) The association shall serve upon the respondent a "Notice of Commencement of Legal Proceedings." The notice shall be served by certified mail to the registered agent of the respondent, or if there is no registered agent, then to any officer of the respondent. If there are no current officers of the respondent, service shall be upon the person or entity otherwise authorized by law to receive service of process. Service upon the general contractor shall be sufficient to initiate the process set forth in this section with regard to any builder or developer, if the builder or developer is not amenable to service of process by the foregoing methods. This notice shall toll all applicable statutes of limitation and repose, whether contractual or statutory, by and against all potentially responsible parties, regardless of whether they were named in the notice, including claims for indemnity applicable to the claim for the period set forth in subdivision (c). The notice shall include all of the following:

(1) The name and location of the project.

(2) An initial list of defects sufficient to apprise the respondent of the general nature of the defects at issue.

(3) A description of the results of the defects, if known.

(4) A summary of the results of a survey or questionnaire distributed to homeowners to determine the nature and extent of defects, if a survey has been conducted or a questionnaire has been distributed.

(5) Either a summary of the results of testing conducted to determine the nature and extent of defects or the actual test results, if that testing has been conducted.

(c) Service of the notice shall commence a period, not to exceed 180 days, during which the association, the respondent, and all other participating parties shall try to resolve the dispute through the processes set forth in this section. This 180-day period may be extended for one additional period, not to exceed 180 days, only upon the mutual agreement of the association, the respondent, and any parties not deemed peripheral pursuant to paragraph (3) of subdivision (e). Any extensions beyond the first extension shall require the agreement of all participating parties. Unless extended, the dispute resolution process prescribed by this section shall be deemed completed. All extensions shall continue the tolling period described in subdivision (b).

(d) Within 25 days of the date the association serves the Notice of Commencement of Legal Proceedings, the respondent may request in writing to meet and confer with the board. Unless the respondent and the association otherwise agree, there shall be not more than one meeting, which shall take place no later than 10 days from the date of the respondent's written request, at a mutually agreeable time and place. The meeting shall be subject to subdivision (a) of Section 4925 and subdivisions (a) and (b) of Section 4935. The discussions at the meeting are privileged communications and are not admissible in evidence in any civil action, unless the association and the respondent consent in writing to their admission.

(e) Upon receipt of the notice, the respondent shall, within 60 days, comply with the following:

(1) The respondent shall provide the association with access to, for inspection and copying of, all plans and specifications, subcontracts, and other construction files for the project that are reasonably calculated to lead to the discovery of admissible evidence regarding the defects claimed. The association shall provide the respondent with access to, for inspection and copying of, all files reasonably calculated to lead to the discovery of admissible evidence regarding

the defects claimed, including all reserve studies, maintenance records and any survey questionnaires, or results of testing to determine the nature and extent of defects. To the extent any of the above documents are withheld based on privilege, a privilege log shall be prepared and submitted to all other parties. All other potentially responsible parties shall have the same rights as the respondent regarding the production of documents upon receipt of written notice of the claim, and shall produce all relevant documents within 60 days of receipt of the notice of the claim.

(2) The respondent shall provide written notice by certified mail to all subcontractors, design professionals, their insurers, and the insurers of any additional insured whose identities are known to the respondent or readily ascertainable by review of the project files or other similar sources and whose potential responsibility appears on the face of the notice. This notice to subcontractors, design professionals, and insurers shall include a copy of the Notice of Commencement of Legal Proceedings, and shall specify the date and manner by which the parties shall meet and confer to select a dispute resolution facilitator pursuant to paragraph (1) of subdivision (f), advise the recipient of its obligation to participate in the meet and confer or serve a written acknowledgment of receipt regarding this notice, advise the recipient that it will waive any challenge to selection of the dispute resolution facilitator if it elects not to participate in the meet and confer, advise the recipient that it may seek the assistance of an attorney, and advise the recipient that it should contact its insurer, if any. Any subcontractor or design professional, or insurer for that subcontractor, design professional, or additional insured, who receives written notice from the respondent regarding the meet and confer shall, prior to the meet and confer, serve on the respondent a written acknowledgment of receipt. That subcontractor or design professional shall, within 10 days of service of the written acknowledgment of receipt, provide to the association and the respondent a Statement of Insurance that includes both of the following:

(A) The names, addresses, and contact persons, if known, of all insurance carriers, whether primary or excess and regardless of whether a deductible or self-insured retention applies, whose policies were in effect from the commencement of construction of the subject project to the present and which potentially cover the subject claims.

(B) The applicable policy numbers for each policy of insurance provided.

(3) Any subcontractor or design professional, or insurer for that subcontractor, design professional, or additional insured, who so chooses, may, at any time, make a written request to the dispute resolution facilitator for designation as a peripheral party. That request shall be served contemporaneously on the association and the respondent. If no objection to that designation is received within 15 days, or upon rejection of that objection, the dispute resolution facilitator shall designate that subcontractor or design professional as a peripheral party, and shall thereafter seek to limit the attendance of that subcontractor or design professional only to those dispute resolution sessions

deemed peripheral party sessions or to those sessions during which the dispute resolution facilitator believes settlement as to peripheral parties may be finalized. Nothing in this subdivision shall preclude a party who has been designated a peripheral party from being reclassified as a nonperipheral party, nor shall this subdivision preclude a party designated as a nonperipheral party from being reclassified as a peripheral party after notice to all parties and an opportunity to object. For purposes of this subdivision, a peripheral party is a party having total claimed exposure of less than twenty-five thousand dollars ($25,000).

(f)(1) Within 20 days of sending the notice set forth in paragraph (2) of subdivision (e), the association, respondent, subcontractors, design professionals, and their insurers who have been sent a notice as described in paragraph (2) of subdivision (e) shall meet and confer in an effort to select a dispute resolution facilitator to preside over the mandatory dispute resolution process prescribed by this section. Any subcontractor or design professional who has been given timely notice of this meeting but who does not participate, waives any challenge he or she may have as to the selection of the dispute resolution facilitator. The role of the dispute resolution facilitator is to attempt to resolve the conflict in a fair manner. The dispute resolution facilitator shall be sufficiently knowledgeable in the subject matter and be able to devote sufficient time to the case. The dispute resolution facilitator shall not be required to reside in or have an office in the county in which the project is located. The dispute resolution facilitator and the participating parties shall agree to a date, time, and location to hold a case management meeting of all parties and the dispute resolution facilitator, to discuss the claims being asserted and the scheduling of events under this section. The case management meeting with the dispute resolution facilitator shall be held within 100 days of service of the Notice of Commencement of Legal Proceedings at a location in the county where the project is located. Written notice of the case management meeting with the dispute resolution facilitator shall be sent by the respondent to the association, subcontractors and design professionals, and their insurers who are known to the respondent to be on notice of the claim, no later than 10 days prior to the case management meeting, and shall specify its date, time, and location. The dispute resolution facilitator in consultation with the respondent shall maintain a contact list of the participating parties.

(2) No later than 10 days prior to the case management meeting, the dispute resolution facilitator shall disclose to the parties all matters that could cause a person aware of the facts to reasonably entertain a doubt that the proposed dispute resolution facilitator would be able to resolve the conflict in a fair manner. The facilitator's disclosure shall include the existence of any ground specified in Section 170.1 of the Code of Civil Procedure for disqualification of a judge, any attorney-client relationship the facilitator has or had with any party or lawyer for a party to the dispute resolution process, and any professional or significant personal relationship the facilitator or his or her spouse or minor child living in the household has or had with any party to the dispute resolution

process. The disclosure shall also be provided to any subsequently noticed subcontractor or design professional within 10 days of the notice.

(3) A dispute resolution facilitator shall be disqualified by the court if he or she fails to comply with this subdivision and any party to the dispute resolution process serves a notice of disqualification prior to the case management meeting. If the dispute resolution facilitator complies with this subdivision, he or she shall be disqualified by the court on the basis of the disclosure if any party to the dispute resolution process serves a notice of disqualification prior to the case management meeting.

(4) If the parties cannot mutually agree to a dispute resolution facilitator, then each party shall submit a list of three dispute resolution facilitators. Each party may then strike one nominee from the other parties' list, and petition the court, pursuant to the procedure described in subdivisions (n) and (o), for final selection of the dispute resolution facilitator. The court may issue an order for final selection of the dispute resolution facilitator pursuant to this paragraph.

(5) Any subcontractor or design professional who receives notice of the association's claim without having previously received timely notice of the meet and confer to select the dispute resolution facilitator shall be notified by the respondent regarding the name, address, and telephone number of the dispute resolution facilitator. Any such subcontractor or design professional may serve upon the parties and the dispute resolution facilitator a written objection to the dispute resolution facilitator within 15 days of receiving notice of the claim. Within seven days after service of this objection, the subcontractor or design professional may petition the superior court to replace the dispute resolution facilitator. The court may replace the dispute resolution facilitator only upon a showing of good cause, liberally construed. Failure to satisfy the deadlines set forth in this subdivision shall constitute a waiver of the right to challenge the dispute resolution facilitator.

(6) The costs of the dispute resolution facilitator shall be apportioned in the following manner: one-third to be paid by the association; one-third to be paid by the respondent; and one-third to be paid by the subcontractors and design professionals, as allocated among them by the dispute resolution facilitator. The costs of the dispute resolution facilitator shall be recoverable by the prevailing party in any subsequent litigation pursuant to Section 1032 of the Code of Civil Procedure, provided however that any nonsettling party may, prior to the filing of the complaint, petition the facilitator to reallocate the costs of the dispute resolution facilitator as they apply to any nonsettling party. The determination of the dispute resolution facilitator with respect to the allocation of these costs shall be binding in any subsequent litigation. The dispute resolution facilitator shall take into account all relevant factors and equities between all parties in the dispute resolution process when reallocating costs.

(7) In the event the dispute resolution facilitator is replaced at any time, the case management statement created pursuant to subdivision (h) shall remain in full

force and effect.

(8) The dispute resolution facilitator shall be empowered to enforce all provisions of this section.

(g)(1) No later than the case management meeting, the parties shall begin to generate a data compilation showing the following information regarding the alleged defects at issue:

(A) The scope of the work performed by each potentially responsible subcontractor.

(B) The tract or phase number in which each subcontractor provided goods or services, or both.

(C) The units, either by address, unit number, or lot number, at which each subcontractor provided goods or services, or both.

(2) This data compilation shall be updated as needed to reflect additional information. Each party attending the case management meeting, and any subsequent meeting pursuant to this section, shall provide all information available to that party relevant to this data compilation.

(h) At the case management meeting, the parties shall, with the assistance of the dispute resolution facilitator, reach agreement on a case management statement, which shall set forth all of the elements set forth in paragraphs (1) to (8), inclusive, except that the parties may dispense with one or more of these elements if they agree that it is appropriate to do so. The case management statement shall provide that the following elements shall take place in the following order:

(1) Establishment of a document depository, located in the county where the project is located, for deposit of documents, defect lists, demands, and other information provided for under this section. All documents exchanged by the parties and all documents created pursuant to this subdivision shall be deposited in the document depository, which shall be available to all parties throughout the prefiling dispute resolution process and in any subsequent litigation. When any document is deposited in the document depository, the party depositing the document shall provide written notice identifying the document to all other parties. The costs of maintaining the document depository shall be apportioned among the parties in the same manner as the costs of the dispute resolution facilitator.

(2) Provision of a more detailed list of defects by the association to the respondent after the association completes a visual inspection of the project. This list of defects shall provide sufficient detail for the respondent to ensure that all potentially responsible subcontractors and design professionals are provided with notice of the dispute resolution process. If not already completed

prior to the case management meeting, the Notice of Commencement of Legal Proceedings shall be served by the respondent on all additional subcontractors and design professionals whose potential responsibility appears on the face of the more detailed list of defects within seven days of receipt of the more detailed list. The respondent shall serve a copy of the case management statement, including the name, address, and telephone number of the dispute resolution facilitator, to all the potentially responsible subcontractors and design professionals at the same time.

(3) Nonintrusive visual inspection of the project by the respondent, subcontractors, and design professionals.

(4) Invasive testing conducted by the association, if the association deems appropriate. All parties may observe and photograph any testing conducted by the association pursuant to this paragraph, but may not take samples or direct testing unless, by mutual agreement, costs of testing are shared by the parties.

(5) Provision by the association of a comprehensive demand which provides sufficient detail for the parties to engage in meaningful dispute resolution as contemplated under this section.

(6) Invasive testing conducted by the respondent, subcontractors, and design professionals, if they deem appropriate.

(7) Allowance for modification of the demand by the association if new issues arise during the testing conducted by the respondent, subcontractor, or design professionals.

(8) Facilitated dispute resolution of the claim, with all parties, including peripheral parties, as appropriate, and insurers, if any, present and having settlement authority. The dispute resolution facilitators shall endeavor to set specific times for the attendance of specific parties at dispute resolution sessions. If the dispute resolution facilitator does not set specific times for the attendance of parties at dispute resolution sessions, the dispute resolution facilitator shall permit those parties to participate in dispute resolution sessions by telephone.

(i) In addition to the foregoing elements of the case management statement described in subdivision (h), upon mutual agreement of the parties, the dispute resolution facilitator may include any or all of the following elements in a case management statement: the exchange of consultant or expert photographs; expert presentations; expert meetings; or any other mechanism deemed appropriate by the parties in the interest of resolving the dispute.

(j) The dispute resolution facilitator, with the guidance of the parties, shall at the time the case management statement is established, set deadlines for the occurrence of each event set forth in the case management statement, taking into account such factors as the size and complexity of the case, and the requirement of this section that this dispute resolution process not exceed 180 days absent agreement of the parties to an extension of time.

(k)(1)(A) At a time to be determined by the dispute resolution facilitator, the respondent may submit to the association all of the following:

(i) A request to meet with the board to discuss a written settlement offer.

(ii) A written settlement offer, and a concise explanation of the reasons for the terms of the offer.

(iii) A statement that the respondent has access to sufficient funds to satisfy the conditions of the settlement offer.

(iv) A summary of the results of testing conducted for the purposes of determining the nature and extent of defects, if this testing has been conducted, unless the association provided the respondent with actual test results.

(B) If the respondent does not timely submit the items required by this subdivision, the association shall be relieved of any further obligation to satisfy the requirements of this subdivision only.

(C) No less than 10 days after the respondent submits the items required by this paragraph, the respondent and the board shall meet and confer about the respondent's settlement offer.

(D) If the board rejects a settlement offer presented at the meeting held pursuant to this subdivision, the board shall hold a meeting open to each member of the association. The meeting shall be held no less than 15 days before the association commences an action for damages against the respondent.

(E) No less than 15 days before this meeting is held, a written notice shall be sent to each member of the association specifying all of the following:

(i) That a meeting will take place to discuss problems that may lead to the filing of a civil action, and the time and place of this meeting.

(ii) The options that are available to address the problems, including the filing of a civil action and a statement of the various alternatives that are reasonably foreseeable by the association to pay for those options and whether these payments are expected to be made from the use of reserve account funds or the imposition of regular or special assessments, or emergency assessment increases.

(iii) The complete text of any written settlement offer, and a concise explanation of the specific reasons for the terms of the offer submitted to the board at the meeting held pursuant to subdivision (d) that was received from the respondent.

(F) The respondent shall pay all expenses attributable to sending the settlement offer to all members of the association. The respondent shall also pay the expense of holding the meeting, not to exceed three dollars ($3) per association member.

(G) The discussions at the meeting and the contents of the notice and the items required to be specified in the notice pursuant to subparagraph (E) are privileged communications and are not admissible in evidence in any civil action, unless the association consents to their admission.

(H) No more than one request to meet and discuss a written settlement offer may be made by the respondent pursuant to this subdivision.

(*l*) All defect lists and demands, communications, negotiations, and settlement offers made in the course of the prelitigation dispute resolution process provided by this section shall be inadmissible pursuant to Sections 1119 to 1124, inclusive, of the Evidence Code and all applicable decisional law. This inadmissibility shall not be extended to any other documents or communications which would not otherwise be deemed inadmissible.

(m) Any subcontractor or design professional may, at any time, petition the dispute resolution facilitator to release that party from the dispute resolution process upon a showing that the subcontractor or design professional is not potentially responsible for the defect claims at issue. The petition shall be served contemporaneously on all other parties, who shall have 15 days from the date of service to object. If a subcontractor or design professional is released, and it later appears to the dispute resolution facilitator that it may be a responsible party in light of the current defect list or demand, the respondent shall renotice the party as provided by paragraph (2) of subdivision (e), provide a copy of the current defect list or demand, and direct the party to attend a dispute resolution session at a stated time and location. A party who subsequently appears after having been released by the dispute resolution facilitator shall not be prejudiced by its absence from the dispute resolution process as the result of having been previously released by the dispute resolution facilitator.

(n) Any party may, at any time, petition the superior court in the county where the project is located, upon a showing of good cause, and the court may issue an order, for any of the following, or for appointment of a referee to resolve a dispute regarding any of the following:

(1) To take a deposition of any party to the process, or subpoena a third party for deposition or production of documents, which is necessary to further prelitigation resolution of the dispute.

(2) To resolve any disputes concerning inspection, testing, production of documents, or exchange of information provided for under this section.

(3) To resolve any disagreements relative to the timing or contents of the case management statement.

(4) To authorize internal extensions of timeframes set forth in the case management statement.

(5) To seek a determination that a settlement is a good faith settlement pursuant to Section 877.6 of the Code of Civil Procedure and all related authorities. The page limitations and meet and confer requirements specified in this section shall not apply to these motions, which may be made on shortened notice. Instead, these motions shall be subject to other applicable state law, rules of court, and local rules. A determination made by the court pursuant to this motion shall have the same force and effect as the determination of a postfiling application or motion for good faith settlement.

(6) To ensure compliance, on shortened notice, with the obligation to provide a Statement of Insurance pursuant to paragraph (2) of subdivision (e).

(7) For any other relief appropriate to the enforcement of the provisions of this section, including the ordering of parties, and insurers, if any, to the dispute resolution process with settlement authority.

(o)(1) A petition filed pursuant to subdivision (n) shall be filed in the superior court in the county in which the project is located. The court shall hear and decide the petition within 10 days after filing. The petitioning party shall serve the petition on all parties, including the date, time, and location of the hearing no later than five business days prior to the hearing. Any responsive papers shall be filed and served no later than three business days prior to the hearing. Any petition or response filed under this section shall be no more than three pages in length.

(2) All parties shall meet with the dispute resolution facilitator, if one has been appointed and confer in person or by telephone prior to the filing of that petition to attempt to resolve the matter without requiring court intervention.

(p) As used in this section:

(1) "Association" shall have the same meaning as defined in Section 4080.

(2) "Builder" means the declarant, as defined in Section 4130.

(3) "Common interest development" shall have the same meaning as in Section 4100, except that it shall not include developments or projects with less than 20 units.

(q) The alternative dispute resolution process and procedures described in this section shall have no application or legal effect other than as described in this section.

(r) This section shall become operative on July 1, 2002, however it shall not apply to any pending suit or claim for which notice has previously been given.

(s) This section shall become inoperative on July 1, 2017, and, as of January 1, 2018, is repealed, unless a later enacted statute, that becomes operative on or before January 1, 2018, deletes or extends the dates on which it becomes inoperative and is repealed.

The Calderon Process adds many requirements for both the Declarant and an Association. This process is different from the pre-litigation requirements contained in SB800. According to SB800, the Association does not need to comply with duplicative requirements. However, to the extent that Calderon and SB800 do not overlap, an Association does need to comply with the Calderon statute.

### The Conclusion of a Defect Claim Under Calderon

In addition to §6000 of the Davis-Sterling Act, an Association has another requirement at the conclusion of a defect claim. That is set forth in Civil Code §6100

**§ 6100. Settlement agreements regarding alleged defects; notice of resolution to members on record; disclosures**

(a) As soon as is reasonably practicable after the association and the builder have entered into a settlement agreement or the matter has otherwise been resolved regarding alleged defects in the common areas, alleged defects in the separate interests that the association is obligated to maintain or repair, or alleged defects in the separate interests that arise out of, or are integrally related to, defects in the common areas or separate interests that the association is obligated to maintain or repair, where the defects giving rise to the dispute have not been corrected, the association shall, in writing, inform only the members of the association whose names appear on the records of the association that the matter has been resolved, by settlement agreement or other means, and disclose all of the following:

(1) A general description of the defects that the association reasonably believes, as of the date of the disclosure, will be corrected or replaced.

(2) A good faith estimate, as of the date of the disclosure, of when the association believes that the defects identified in paragraph (1) will be corrected or replaced. The association may state that the estimate may be modified.

(3) The status of the claims for defects in the design or construction of the common interest development that were not identified in paragraph (1) whether expressed in a preliminary list of defects sent to each member of the association or otherwise claimed and disclosed to the members of the association.

(b) Nothing in this section shall preclude an association from amending the disclosures required pursuant to subdivision (a), and any amendments shall supersede any prior conflicting information disclosed to the members of the association and shall retain any privilege attached to the original disclosures.

(c) Disclosure of the information required pursuant to subdivision (a) or authorized by subdivision (b) shall not waive any privilege attached to the information.

(d) For the purposes of the disclosures required pursuant to this section, the term "defects" shall be defined to include any damage resulting from defects.

Essentially, an Association must inform its members at the conclusion of a defect claim. The information should include the issues litigated and the outcome. In addition, the Association has an ongoing obligation to inform its members about repairs that are being made and that are anticipated to be made.

Funds from a construction defect action should be separated from the general operating fund as well as from the reserve accounts. Funds from construction defects are to be used to make repairs.

Finally, it is important to remember that decisions about what to repair and what to not repair is not a subject for Executive Session. The negotiation of a contract can be in Executive Session but the discussion about what to repair and the order of what to repair is a subject for the membership to hear if they choose to attend the meeting.

# Chapter 7

# Arbitration, Mediation and Trials – What is the Difference?

A question that is often asked by clients is what is the difference between Arbitration, Mediation and a Trial. This chapter will answer this question.

## What is Mediation?

Mediation is a "settlement conference" or a meeting that allows the parties to make a decision. The decision – whether to accept a settlement or not. A mediation is usually handled at a neutral location – a mediation facility or a court reporter's office. The parties may or may not meet together for what is often referred to as a "joint session."

In general, mediation is an opportunity to share information and positions. It is up to the parties with the advice of their counsel whether they want to accept an offer that is made or counter with a different offer.

In construction defect cases it is very common to have 3 or more mediation sessions. The mediations often are information sharing sessions at the beginning. The final mediation session is often about money and how much will be paid.

Mediation gives the parties 100% control. In an Arbitration or a Trial, the parties give up control on the outcome and leave that decision to either a Judge or a Jury.

## What is an Arbitration?

Often confused with Mediation, Arbitration is not a Mediation at all. An Arbitration is a private trial. Instead of having a courtroom assigned to you in the Superior Court with a Jury chosen from those serving Jury Duty, the parties choose a "Neutral" to act as the Judge and Jury.

The Neutral is often a retired Judge but that is not always the case. Sometimes lawyers become Arbitrators or Neutrals. The key is that the parties or more often their lawyers choose the Neutral. Generally, the Neutral will be chosen based upon prior experience in the subject matter of your case.

In some situations, an Arbitration clause will require that both parties choose a Neutral. The two chosen Neutrals will then choose a third Neutral.

The cost of the Neutral is paid for by the parties. Some Arbitration clauses provide that the Arbitration will be paid for by the Builder. Some clauses provide that the Arbitrator can re-allocate the cost of the Neutral at the conclusion of the Arbitration depending on the outcome of the claim.

The decision to Arbitrate or Litigate (a trial) is generally made before a lawyer is hired by a homeowner or an Association. The decision is often in the purchase agreement and/or the Association's Governing Documents – its CC&Rs. Following the *Pinnacle* decision, this provision can be enforceable – depending on the terms of the clause.

Once the Arbitration is completed, the Arbitrator will issue a written decision. That decision can be issued in a matter of days or weeks. The decision of an Arbitrator is generally not subject to an appeal. Sometimes an Arbitrator's decision can be appealed – that is dependent upon the Arbitration Agreement between the parties.

## What is a Trial?

A trial is a public way to have a decision about your case made. Often construction defect cases are tried using a Jury but sometimes a Judge can be the sole decision maker. A trial occurs in the Court as opposed to a private conference room (where mediation and arbitration takes place).

The Judge assigned to your case will be random. In many counties, there are specific judges that are assigned to handle complex construction defect cases. They are deemed complex by the Courts because of the number of parties as well as the number of issues that are often presented.

If you have a Jury, the members that serve on that Jury are selected at random from the Jury Pool. Those who are serving Jury Duty on the date your jury selection begins will be pre-screened for the length of your trial. From that group, you will begin jury selection.

Once you have presented your case to the Jury, the Jury will meet in private and use the Verdict Form that it is given by the Court to make its decision. The parties wait for the decision that can take hours or days.

Jury verdicts are subject to appeal. Also, decisions or rulings of the Judge during the trial are also subject to appeal. Thus, a decision at the conclusion of the trial may or may not be the end of your case.

# Chapter 8

# Conclusion

As you can see, the handling of a construction defect claim can be very complex. This is why most claims of this type are handled by attorneys who practice in this area of law.

Homeowners and Associations can get themselves into trouble when they try to handle these types of claims on their own or with counsel who does not regularly handle construction defect cases.

Before embarking on an SB800 claim on your own or with inexperienced counsel, it is generally well worth the time to consult with a construction defect attorney. Often you will learn much more about the claim process and your individual claim in that consultation.

At Scott D. Levine, APC we will visit your property with our team of experts at no charge and without obligation. We will meet with you as well. The goal of our visit and our meeting is to make sure that your project requires our help and that we are the right firm to help you in your individual situation. If we can help you, we will let you know. Likewise, if we cannot help you, we will let you know that as well. You have nothing to lose by contacting our office as there is no obligation if you do not wish to work with us after you have met with us.

# About the Author

Scott Levine has been representing homeowners and homeowner associations since the early 1990s when he became an attorney. He began his practice representing developers – not in construction defect cases but in general civil litigation matters. One day he was asked by another associate in the law firm that he worked to sit in on a construction defect deposition. From that point forward, Scott has worked on construction defect cases.

The complexity and dynamics of the people and issues has drawn Scott to enjoy helping homeowners and homeowner associations through the maze of what is construction defect litigation. Before the *Aas* decision was handed down by the California Supreme Court, the practice was fair to homeowners and homeowner associations. When the Court issued its decision, Scott knew that the only remedy for consumers in California was to seek legislation that fixed what the Court did to them.

In 2002, Scott had the distinguished opportunity to work on legislation that became what is known today as SB800 or Civil Code §895 et seq. The negotiations came during the summer of 2002 and occupied a great deal of Scott's time and energy. In the end though, consumers were given a set of standards that they could hold builders responsible for in the construction of their homes and buildings. The trade was a right to repair – a right that most builders do not take seriously.

Since 2002, Scott has lectured with lawyers who practice construction defect litigation as well as with mediators, retired judges and sitting judges on the subject. These lectures have given Scott insight into the practice from different perspectives. This allows Scott to provide advice knowing that there is another side to the case. Sometimes that advice is to mediate and other times it is to fight on for another period of time.

Scott enjoys working with homeowners and homeowner

associations to educate them about the law and about their particular case. No two cases are the same and each client or group of clients in the case of single family homes deserves a litigation strategy that is best for them and their situation.

We honor the opportunity to meet with you and to discuss your concerns. Give us a call!